C000000560

KITCHEN
RECIPES

compiled by
Carole Gregory

*illustrated with
farmyard scenes by*
Michael Cooper

SALMON BOOKS

Index

Belly Pork with Red Cabbage 6
Blackberry Cordial 46
Brown Bread Ice Cream 31
Buttermilk Cake 39
Cheesy Leeks with Ham 16
Chicken and Apple Cheesebake 21
Cock-a-Leekie 22
Country Chicken 7
Damson Chutney 45
Date and Walnut Cake 35
Egg, Bacon and Leek Pie 5
Elderflower Champagne 47
Farmhouse Chicken Casserole 3
Fruit Gingerbread 40
Gingerbread Men 43
Ginger Griddle Scones 34
Gloucestershire Pie 15

Gooseberry Flan 32
Ham and Cheese Toasties 14
Kidney and Sausage Casserole 13
Lemon Dessert 27
Minced Beef Casserole 18
Mushroom Soup 23
Oat Squares 42
Picnic Pasty 10
Raspberry Cake 30
Sausage Pie 19
Shortbread Biscuits 38
Smoked Haddock Flan 11
Sultana Cake 37
Summer Pudding 29
Summer Soup 26
Turkey Broth 24
Turkey Pie 8

Cover pictures *front:* 'Counting Sheep'
back: 'Seymour's Farm'
title page: 'Please Shut the Gate'

Printed and Published by Dorrigo, Manchester, England © Copyright

Farmhouse Chicken Casserole

*A simple casserole dish based upon chicken joints with baby onions
and small new potatoes.*

**4 large chicken joints   1 oz. seasoned flour   2 oz. butter
1½ lb. small new potatoes, scraped
1 clove garlic, crushed   12 baby onions, peeled
4 rashers streaky bacon, de-rinded and diced
4 sticks celery, washed and sliced   4 oz. button mushrooms
1 pint chicken stock   1 heaped teaspoon dried mixed herbs   1 teaspoon paprika
Salt and black pepper   1 bayleaf
Chopped parsley for garnish**

Set oven to 350°F or Mark 4. Toss the chicken joints in seasoned flour. Melt the butter in a frying pan and brown the joints in the butter until golden all over. Place the joints in a large casserole dish and add the potatoes. Put the garlic, onions, bacon, celery and mushrooms in the pan and cook for a few minutes. Add the remainder of the flour and stir in well. Add the stock gradually, stirring constantly. Add the herbs and paprika and check the seasoning. Pour over the chicken and potatoes in the casserole. Add the bayleaf. Cover and cook for about 1 to 1¼ hours until tender. Remove the bayleaf and garnish with parsley. Serve with carrots. Serves 4.

THE OLD LANDY

Egg, Bacon and Leek Pie

Whole eggs are cooked within this tasty, shallow leek and bacon pie.

6 oz. shortcrust pastry
4 oz. leeks, washed and very thinly sliced
6 oz. streaky bacon, de-rinded and diced   4 eggs
Salt and black pepper
Pinch of freshly grated nutmeg

Set oven to 400°F or Mark 6. Grease a 7 inch round deep flan dish. Roll out the pastry on a floured surface and use about two-thirds to line the dish. Place the thinly sliced leeks on the pastry, then a layer of bacon pieces and lastly break the 4 eggs on top. Season, sprinkle over the nutmeg, cover with a thin layer of pastry and seal the edge. Bake for about 40 minutes until the pastry is golden brown. Serve hot with a green vegetable or cold with chutney and salad. Serves 4.

Belly Pork with Red Cabbage

This flavoursome mixture of pork, apple and red cabbage goes well with baked potatoes and a collation of cold meats.

1 lb. belly pork, de-rinded and cut into cubes   2 tablespoons dripping
4 oz. lean bacon, diced   1 small onion, finely chopped
1 large cooking apple, peeled, cored and diced
Pinch of dried mixed herbs   Pinch each of ground nutmeg and pepper
¼ pint chicken stock   3 level tablespoons sugar   3 level tablespoons wine vinegar
1 medium red cabbage, finely shredded   Rind and juice of 1 orange

Set oven to 300°F or Mark 2. Melt the dripping in a large saucepan and add the pork, bacon, onion and apple. Stir for a few minutes over a gentle heat and sprinkle with herbs and spices. Mix together the stock, sugar and vinegar. Meanwhile wash the cabbage well in salted water. Put the shredded cabbage and orange rind and juice in the pan and mix all the ingredients well. Add the liquid and transfer the whole to a large buttered casserole dish. Cover and cook in the oven for about 2 hours. Remove the orange peel. Serves 4.

Country Chicken

A simple chicken casserole with mushrooms, celery and frozen peas.

4 large chicken joints   2 oz. butter
2 onions, peeled and thinly sliced
6 medium size potatoes, peeled and cubed
½ head celery, chopped   ¼ lb. mushrooms, sliced
Salt and black pepper   Pinch ground nutmeg
1 tablespoon chopped fresh parsley   1 bayleaf
½ pint chicken stock   4 oz. packet frozen peas

Set oven to 350°F or Mark 4. Skin the chicken joints. Melt the butter in a pan and fry the joints until golden brown. Transfer to a warmed casserole dish. Next fry the onions until soft but not browned and then add all the other ingredients to the pan except the peas. Return to the heat and when heated through pour over the chicken in the casserole. Cover and cook in the oven for 30 minutes. Add the peas and cook for a further 15 minutes. Serves 4.

Turkey Pie

An easily made dish, rather like a cottage pie, which uses
left-over cooked turkey. Useful after Christmas.

1 lb. cooked turkey, diced
1 small onion, peeled and chopped   2 oz. butter
4 oz. sweetcorn kernels (frozen or tinned)
1 tablespoon chopped parsley or chives   Black pepper
15 oz. tin condensed soup (choice optional)   1 tablespoon sherry
1½ lb. mashed potato beaten with 1 small egg

Set oven to 325°F or Mark 3. First peel the potatoes and cook in salted water to make the mash. Meanwhile, melt the butter in a pan and fry the onion for a few minutes to soften, but not brown. Stir in the diced turkey, sweetcorn and herbs and season with pepper. Gradually stir in the soup and sherry over a low heat and continue stirring until heated through. Transfer to an ovenproof dish. Mash the potatoes and beat in the egg. Top the dish with mashed potato and cook in the oven for 30 to 40 minutes until browned on top. Serve with a green vegetable and chutney. Serves 4.

STILL WORKING

Picnic Pasty

Cold cooked meat or corned beef form the basis of this large, flat pasty which can be cut into squares or slices to suit individual appetites.

12 oz. shortcrust pastry
1 large onion, peeled and finely chopped
1 large potato, peeled and diced
1 large carrot, peeled and diced
4 oz. runner beans or celery, chopped
Seasoning to taste   Pinch of dried mixed herbs
8 oz. cold cooked meat or corned beef, chopped
2 tablespoons gravy or stock

Set oven to 400°F or Mark 6. Grease a 10 x 12 inch shallow baking tin. Put the onion, potato, carrot and beans or celery in a saucepan. Cover with boiling water and cook for 5 minutes. Meanwhile roll out the pastry on a lightly floured surface and line the base and sides of the tin with a little more than half the pastry. Drain the vegetables, add the seasoning, herbs, cooked meat or corned beef, gravy or stock and mix well. Cover the pastry with filling, brush the edges with water and cover with a layer of pastry. Pinch and seal the edges. Brush the top with milk and bake for about 40 minutes until golden. Eat hot or cold cut into squares or slices. Serve with chutney and salad.

Smoked Haddock Flan

Flaked haddock with hard-boiled eggs in a cheesy sauce, with piped creamy mashed potato.

6 oz. shortcrust pastry
1½ lb. smoked haddock, cooked and flaked
1 small onion, thinly sliced   2 hard boiled eggs, sliced
¾ oz. butter   2 oz. grated Cheddar cheese   1 tablespoon flour
½ pint milk (infused with slice of onion, herbs, bayleaf and peppercorns)
1½-2 lb. cooked creamed mashed potato   Salt and pepper

Set oven to 400°F or Mark 6. Grease an 8 inch loose-bottom flan tin. Roll out the pastry on a floured surface, line the tine and trim the edge. Boil the peeled potatoes in salted water. Meanwhile cook the fish gently for a few minutes in water in a frying pan. Allow the fish to cool, remove the skin and flake the flesh. Arrange the fish in the flan, cover with the onion and place the slices of hard-boiled egg around the edge. Melt the butter in a small pan, stir in the flour and blend in ½ pint of the strained infused milk. Add the cheese, season and stir constantly over a gentle heat until the sauce thickens. Spoon the sauce over the flan. Mash the potatoes and cream with a little butter and milk. Put the mashed potato in a piping bag with a large rose nozzle and pipe around the edge of the flan and across the centre in a lattice pattern. Cook in the oven for 20 to 30 minutes until browned. Serves 4 to 5.

SEYMOUR'S FARM

Kidney and Sausage Casserole

The sautéed lamb's kidneys lift this dish above the level a more usual sausage stew.

6 lamb's kidneys	1 tablespoon tomato purée
1 oz. flour	½ pint brown stock
1 oz. butter	2 tablespoons dry sherry
12 baby onions	4 oz. frozen peas
¼ lb. button mushrooms	½ lb. cocktail sausages

Salt and pepper

Set oven to 325°F or Mark 3. Heat the butter in a pan, gently fry the onions and mushrooms for 5 minutes, then transfer to a casserole dish. Skin the kidneys, cut them in half and remove the core. Dredge them in the flour and sauté gently for a few minutes. Add the tomato purée, stock and sherry to the pan and mix well; pour into the casserole dish and season. Cover and cook for about 20 minutes, then add the peas and cook for a further 25 minutes until the kidneys are tender. Meanwhile grill or sauté the sausages (chippolatas cut in half can be used if necessary) until they are golden brown and add to the dish. Serve with potatoes and a vegetable. Serves 6.

Ham and Cheese Toasties

A superior form of cheese on toast.

4 slices bread
4 thin slices cooked ham
1 tablespoon of chutney (to favoured choice)
4 oz. grated cheese
1 small beaten egg
Black pepper
4 tomatoes halved and grilled
Paprika to decorate   Watercress sprigs to garnish

Pre-heat the grill. Toast the bread on one side only. Butter the untoasted side and place a slice of ham on each slice of bread. Spread a layer of the favoured chutney over the ham. Mix the cheese, egg and pepper together and spread evenly over the chutney. Place under a hot grill until the cheese melts and is golden brown. Sprinkle paprika over the top and garnish with two halves of grilled tomatoes and a sprig of watercress to each plate. Serve with sprinkled Worcestershire Sauce. Serves 4.

Gloucestershire Pie

A variation of shepherd's pie using slices of cooked lamb rather than mince, and including sliced cooking apples.

1 lb. lean lamb, cooked and sliced
1 lb. onions, peeled and thinly sliced
1 lb. cooking apples, peeled, cored and thinly sliced
½-¾ lb. swede, peeled and diced   ½-¾ lb. potatoes, peeled and diced
2 oz. butter   Salt and pepper
Pinch each of dried rosemary and ground nutmeg
½ pint rich gravy or thickened stock

Set oven to 375°F or Mark 5. Put the onions and apples in a saucepan, cover with water and bring to the boil. Boil for 5 minutes and drain well. Meanwhile boil the swede for 10 minutes, then add the potatoes and cook until both are soft. Drain well and mash together until smooth. Grease an ovenproof dish with the butter. Place layers of meat, onion and apple in the dish, seasoning and sprinkling each layer with herbs as the dish is filled up. Pour in the gravy and top with the mashed potato and swede mixture. Spread evenly with a fork, dot with butter and bake, uncovered, for ¾ to 1 hour until browned on top. Serve with a green vegetable. Serves 4.

Cheesy Leeks with Ham

A simple light supper dish. If the leeks are too long, use four cut in half.

8 young leeks   8 thin slices cooked ham
1½ oz. butter   ½ oz. flour
½ pint milk   ¼ pint water, reserved from cooking leeks
6 oz. grated Cheddar cheese
1 teaspoon made English mustard
Salt and black pepper

Well butter a shallow, ovenproof dish. Wash the leeks well and cook in salted boiling water until tender. Drain well, reserving ¼ pint water for the sauce. Wrap a slice of ham around each leek and place in the ovenproof dish and keep warm. Melt the butter in a small pan, stir in the flour and cook for 1 minute. Remove from the heat and gradually stir in the milk and reserved leek stock. Return to the heat and stir constantly until the mixture thickens. Stir in 4 oz. of the grated cheese and the mustard and seasoning. Pour the sauce over the leeks. Sprinkle with the remaining grated cheese and place the dish under a hot grill until it is brown and bubbling. Serve with wholemeal bread. Serves 4.

MARCUS' BARN

Minced Beef Casserole

A dish that is best made the day before it is required, so as to improve the flavour.

2 lb. lean minced beef	2 large onions, sliced
3 tablespoons seasoned flour	4 oz. swede or turnip, cubed
3 tablespoons cooking oil	2 pints water and 2 beef stock cubes
2 oz. mushrooms, sliced	1 small can tomatoes
4 carrots, cubed	Pinch of mixed herbs
2 sticks celery, sliced	Salt and pepper

2 teaspoons brown sugar

Set oven to 300°F or Mark 2. Heat the oil in large frying pan. Mix the meat with the seasoned flour and fry until well browned. Transfer to a casserole dish. Put the fresh vegetables the frying pan, cover and sweat for a few minutes; then add the rest of the ingredients and mix well. Check the seasoning. Pour over the meat in the casserole and stir well. Cover tightly and cook slowly for about 1½ hours. Serve with French fried potatoes and a green vegetable. Serves 6 to 8.

Sausage Pie

*This pie made with sausage meat is very adaptable. It can be eaten hot or cold
and is a very useful addition to the picnic hamper.*

8 oz. shortcrust pastry	1 level teaspoon chopped parsley
¾ lb. pork sausage meat	2 tablespoons chicken stock
1 small onion, finely chopped	1 small beaten egg
1 level teaspoon chopped chives	Salt and black pepper

Set oven to 375°F or Mark 5. Grease an 8 inch ovenproof pie dish. Roll out
the pastry on a floured surface and use two-thirds to line the pie dish. In a
bowl, and using only half the quantity of beaten egg, mix together all the
ingredients very well with a fork. Place the mixture in the pie dish and level
off. Top with a pastry lid and trim and flute the edges with the back of a knife;
make a steam hole in the centre. Glaze the pastry with the remaining beaten
egg. Bake for 15 minutes then reduce oven to 325°F or Mark 3 and continue
baking for 30 to 45 minutes until the pie is cooked through. Serve hot with
vegetables or cold with salad. Serves 4 to 6.

THRESHING DAY

Chicken and Apple Cheesebake

An unusual supper dish with a crispy topping finished with buttered apple slices.

12 oz. cooked chicken, diced
5 Cox's Orange Pippin apples
4 oz. butter
½ pint white sauce
4 oz. grated Cheddar cheese
4 tablespoons toasted white breadcrumbs
Salt and black pepper

Set oven to 400°F or Mark 6. Butter a shallow ovenproof dish. Peel, core and slice 4 of the apples and fry them gently in the butter. Arrange the chicken pieces in the bottom of the dish and arrange the apple slices on top. Make ½ pint of white sauce. Mix 3 oz. of cheese into the white sauce and pour over the apples. Season. Mix the breadcrumbs with the remaining 1 oz. of cheese and sprinkle over the sauce. Core the one remaining apple, cut into rings (unpeeled) and toss in the left-over apple butter. Arrange neatly on top of the dish. Bake for 20 to 30 minutes until crisp and golden. Serves 4.

Cock-a-Leekie

More than a soup – a traditional Scottish speciality.

One 2½ lb. oven-ready fresh chicken
1 lb. leeks, trimmed and sliced
2 pints hot water and 2 chicken stock cubes
Bouquet garni
Salt and freshly ground black pepper
12 no-soak prunes (optional)
A little cornflour to thicken
Chopped fresh parsley to garnish

Put the chicken with the leeks into a large saucepan. Dissolve the stock cubes in the water and add to the pan with the *bouquet garni*. Bring to the boil and remove any scum. Cover the pan and simmer very gently for 1 to 1½ hours until the chicken is tender. Remove the chicken from the pan, skin it and cut the meat into neat pieces. Return the meat to the pan and season to taste. If using prunes, add now and simmer for a further 20 minutes. Thicken with a little cornflour mixed to a cream with water and add the chopped parsley. The flavour improves if this dish is made the day before it is required. Serves 4.

Mushroom Soup

Home-made mushroom soup tastes so much better than the normal tinned varieties.

8 oz. large flat mushrooms, finely chopped
2 medium onions, peeled and very finely chopped
2 oz. butter   2 oz. flour
2 pints strongly flavoured chicken stock
1 tablespoon rice   1 bayleaf   Salt and pepper
1 tablespoon dry sherry
Chopped leaves of lemon balm to garnish

Wipe the mushrooms with a damp cloth. Do not peel, but chop them very finely.   Melt 1 oz. butter in a frying pan, add the chopped onion and mushrooms and cook for a few minutes, covered. Remove the lid, add the rest of the butter and, when melted, stir in the flour and the stock. Add the rice, bayleaf and seasoning. Simmer very gently for 20 minutes until the rice is tender. Remove the bayleaf and check the seasoning. Add the sherry, re-heat and serve hot, garnished with chopped lemon balm (or a herb of your choice). Serves 4 to 6.

Turkey Broth

This sustaining soup is a useful means of using up the remains of a roast turkey.

2 oz. butter   1 onion, finely chopped
1 large carrot, finely cubed   8 oz. potato, peeled and cubed
1 stick celery, chopped   8 oz. cooked turkey, diced
4 oz. peas   4 oz. runner beans, sliced
1 oz. flour   Pinch of dried mixed herbs
1 teaspoon curry powder
1½ pints chicken stock
½ pint creamy milk   Salt and pepper
Chopped fresh parsley   Paprika to garnish

Melt the butter in a large saucepan, add all the vegetables except the peas and beans and fry gently for a few minutes to soften. Stir in the curry powder and cook for a few minutes. Add the flour, mix in and gradually stir in the stock. Add the herbs, bring to the boil, cover and simmer gently for 40 minutes. Add the peas, beans and turkey meat and simmer for 15 minutes, then add the milk and chopped parsley and season to taste. When hot, serve with a sprinkle of paprika on top of each bowl. Serves 6.

FEEDING TIME

Summer Soup

A chilled soup made with the freshest of summer vegetables.

**2 oz. butter   1 onion, finely chopped
1 rasher of bacon, cut into pieces
½ cucumber, peeled and cubed   1 medium potato, cubed
2 large heads of lettuce, cleaned and shredded
2 oz. flour   Salt and pepper
Pinch of dried mixed herbs   ¾ pint chicken or ham stock
¾ pint milk   Croûtons to garnish**

Melt the butter in a large saucepan, add the onion, bacon, cucumber and potato and fry gently for a few minutes to soften. Mix well. Add the lettuce, cover and cook for 5 minutes more. Sprinkle in the flour and seasoning, and mix. Add the herbs and stock and mix together. Bring to the boil and when the mixture thickens add the milk and simmer gently until the potato is cooked. Blend together in a food processor or use a potato masher. Return to the pan, heat through and serve with fried croûtons. Serves 4 to 6.

Lemon Dessert

This cream covered, lemon flavoured gateau makes a party treat.

1 packet trifle sponges or 1 home-made fatless sponge
4 oz. soft margarine   4 oz. caster sugar
4 eggs, separated   2 large lemons
¼ pint double cream
5 glacé cherries   5 chocolate squares

Well butter a 1 lb. loaf tin. Cream the margarine and sugar together in a bowl until fluffy. Add the egg yolks. Whisk the egg whites until stiff and fold into the mixture, then add the grated rind and juice of the 2 lemons. Do not worry if the mixture curdles. Cut the sponges lengthways and put a layer of sponge on the base of the tin then add a layer of lemon mixture, continuing alternately and finishing with a layer of sponge on top. Cover with kitchen foil and put in the refrigerator for 24 hours. When required, turn out on to a flat serving dish. Completely cover with whipped cream and decorate the top with a line of cherries and chocolate squares, placed alternately. Serve chilled. Serves 5 to 6.

COUNTING SHEEP

Summer Pudding

This delicious and quintessentially English cold pudding consists of a bread lining soaked with lightly cooked and juicy summer soft fruits.

1–1½ lb. fruit (a mixture of raspberries, strawberries, redcurrants, blackcurrants etc)
Sugar to taste   Scant ¼ pint water
4-6 slices medium sliced bread
5 oz. whipped cream

Take a 2 pint pudding basin. Put the currants with sufficient sugar to taste into a pan with the water. Simmer gently until almost soft, add the raspberries and strawberries and cook for a further 3 minutes. Meanwhile cut the crusts off the bread and then cut the bread to fit the base and sides of the basin. Put the fruit mixture into the basin, reserving 2-3 ozs. juice. Top with the remaining bread, pressing down firmly. Cover the basin with a saucer to fit the top exactly, place about a 1 lb weight on top and leave in the refrigerator overnight. Turn out on to a serving dish just before serving and use the reserved juice to cover any parts of the bread which have remained white. Serve with whipped cream. Serves 4 to 6.

Raspberry Cake

A luscious sandwich cake filled with fresh raspberries and whipped cream.

4 oz. soft margarine   4 oz. caster sugar
5 oz. self-raising flour
1 packet raspberry flavoured blanc-mange powder
2 eggs, beaten   1 tablespoon warm water
½ lb. fresh raspberries   5 oz. whipped cream

Set oven to 375°F or Mark 5. Grease and line two 7 inch round sandwich tins. Cream the margarine and sugar together in a bowl until fluffy then beat in the eggs, flour and blanc-mange powder, add the warm water and mix well. Put half the mixture into each of the tins and bake for about 20 minutes until firm. Turn out onto a wire rack to cool and, when cold, sandwich with whipped cream and raspberries sweetened to taste.

Brown Bread Ice Cream

A delicious frozen, rum-flavoured concoction of brown breadcrumbs and whipped cream.

½ **pint double cream**	**4 oz. brown breadcrumbs**
¼ **pint single cream**	**2 eggs, separated**
3 oz. sifted icing sugar	**1 tablespoon rum**

Whisk the double cream until stiff and then gradually whisk in the single cream. Fold in the sugar and breadcrumbs. Whisk together the egg yolks and rum and fold into the mixture. Lastly, beat the egg whites until stiff and fold in carefully with a metal spoon. Turn the mixture into a freezer-proof container and freeze for at least 4 hours before serving. Serves 6.

Gooseberry Flan

A truly superior fruit dessert.

6 oz. shortcrust pastry
1 lb. gooseberries, topped and tailed
2 heads of elderflower, cleaned
6 tablespoons white wine
4 tablespoons clear honey, warmed
2 beaten eggs   Pinch of ground nutmeg   Pinch of salt
¼ pint double cream

Set oven to 375°F or Mark 5. Grease an 8 inch loose-bottom flan tin. Roll out the pastry on a floured surface, line the tin and trim the edge. Meanwhile, put the gooseberries in a saucepan with the elderflower heads and the wine. Cover and simmer very gently until the fruit is tender; this takes about 20 minutes. Remove the elderflowers. Stir the mixture and beat well with a fork then rub through a sieve into a clean bowl. Add the warmed honey then the beaten eggs, nutmeg, salt and cream. Mix well and pour into the pastry case. Bake for about 40 minutes until firm and golden brown. Serve chilled with a jug of cream. Serves 6.

THE OLD FIELD MARSHALL

Ginger Griddle Scones

These ginger-flavoured scones are delicious eaten warm,
split and spread thickly with butter.

8 oz. plain flour   1 level teaspoon bicarbonate of soda
Pinch of salt   1 level teaspoon ground ginger
2 oz. hard margarine   2 oz. caster sugar
¼ pint of milk   2 level teaspoons cream of tartar

Sift the flour, bicarbonate of soda, salt and ginger into a bowl. Rub in the margarine and stir in the sugar. Dissolve the cream of tartar in the milk and use to bind the mixture to form a soft dough. Knead with floured hands and divide the dough into two portions on a floured surface. Form each portion into a flattened circle and cut into four. Place the 8 scones on a hot griddle or heavy-based frying pan and cook for 5 minutes on each side. Serve warm.

Date and Walnut Cake

A tray-bake covered with a soft butterscotch icing.

8 oz. chopped dates   1 teaspoon bicarbonate of soda
3 oz. butter   8 oz. sugar
1 large egg   1 teaspoon vanilla essence
10 oz. plain flour   1 teaspoon baking powder   ½ teaspoon salt

ICING
2½ tablespoons Demerara sugar   1 tablespoon butter
1 tablespoon cream   Chopped walnuts for decoration

Set oven to 350°F or Mark 4. Grease and line a 12 inch x 9 inch baking tin.
Pour one breakfast cup of boiling water over 8 oz. chopped dates and add
1 teaspoon bicarbonate of soda. Let this stand while mixing the main
ingredients. Cream together the butter and sugar in a bowl. Add the beaten
egg and stir in the vanilla essence. Add the flour, baking powder and salt. Add
the date mixture to the cake mixture and mix well. Put into the tin, spread out
and bake for 40 minutes. When cooked cover with icing. Leave to cool, then
turn out and cut into squares or slices.
ICING – Mix the ingredients in a saucepan. Heat gently to bring to the boil,
and boil for 3 minutes stirring continuously. Allow to cool a little and pour
evenly over the cake. To finish, scatter with chopped walnuts.

SEEN BETTER DAYS

Sultana Cake

*This fruit cake, which includes marmalade in its ingredients,
improves in flavour if left for 48 hours before cutting.*

1 lb. sultanas	2 level teaspoons baking powder
8 oz. butter	Pinch of salt
1 tablespoon marmalade	1 level teaspoon mixed spice
12 oz. plain flour	12 oz. caster sugar

3 beaten eggs

Set oven to 325°F or Mark 3. Grease and line a 10 inch round cake tin. Put the sultanas into a large saucepan and barely cover with cold water. Bring to the boil and boil for 5 minutes. Drain the fruit well and return to the pan. Add the butter cut up into small pieces, to the fruit in the pan. Stir until it has melted and then add the marmalade. Leave to cool. Meanwhile sift the flour, baking powder, salt and spice into a large bowl. Beat the sugar and eggs together well, add to the flour mixture and lastly add the fruit mixture. Blend well and turn into the prepared tin. Bake for 1 hour then lower oven to 300°F or Mark 2 and bake for a further 30 minutes or until a skewer inserted comes out clean. Turn out and cool on a wire rack.

Shortbread Biscuits

A thin, crisp biscuit which is ideal to enjoy at coffee time,
or to accompany fruit desserts.

6 oz. butter
2 oz. icing sugar
8 oz. self-raising flour

Set oven to 350°F or Mark 4. Grease baking sheets. Cream the butter and icing sugar together in a bowl until very soft and fluffy. Gradually stir in the sifted flour and knead lightly. Roll out to ⅛-¼ inch thickness on a lightly floured surface. Cut out the biscuits with a plain or fluted cutter, place on sheets and bake for 8 to 10 minutes until pale brown. Transfer to a wire rack to cool and then sprinkle with sifted icing sugar.

Buttermilk Cake

This rich fruit cake is made with buttermilk to aid the raising and add extra flavour.

4 oz. butter   4 oz. margarine   8 oz. Demerara sugar
3 beaten eggs   1 lb. plain flour
2 level teaspoons baking powder
2 level teaspoons bicarbonate of soda
1 level teaspoon cream of tartar   ¼ level teaspoon salt
¼ level teaspoon ground ginger   1 level teaspoon grated nutmeg
½ pint buttermilk (or use 1 tablespoon vinegar made up to ½ pint with fresh milk)
12 oz. currants   4 oz. sultanas   2 oz. glacé cherries

Set oven to 325°F or Mark 3. Grease and line a 9 inch square cake tin. In a bowl, cream together the butter, margarine and sugar until light and fluffy. Add the eggs, the sifted dry ingredients and the buttermilk. Stir in the fruit and mix well together. Turn the mixture into the tin and bake for 1½ to 2 hours in the centre of the oven until firm and a skewer inserted comes out clean. Leave in the tin for about 5 minutes and turn out on to a wire rack to cool.

Fruit Gingerbread

A traditional gingerbread cake which contains sultanas;
it may be eaten plain or iced with a ginger icing.

6 oz. butter   6 oz. black treacle   6 oz. golden syrup   4 oz. caster sugar
1 lb. plain flour   1 teaspoon ground ginger   1 rounded teaspoon bicarbonate of soda
Pinch of salt   3 oz. sultanas   2 eggs   4 fl.oz. milk

ICING
1 tablespoon warmed golden syrup   8 oz. icing sugar   Warm water
Crystallised ginger to decorate

Set oven to 350°F or Mark 4. Grease and line a 7 inch square cake tin. Melt the butter, treacle, syrup and sugar together gently in a pan. Sift together the flour, ginger and bicarbonate of soda into a bowl. Add the salt and sultanas. Beat the eggs in a separate bowl and add the milk, then add to the flour mixture. To this add the warmed treacle mixture and mix well. Pour into the tin and bake for 45 to 60 minutes until firm and a skewer inserted comes out clean. Cool on a wire rack.

ICING – Warm the syrup in a pan and mix in to the sifted icing sugar. If too thick add drops of warmed water carefully until a dropping consistency is achieved. Spread over the cake and decorate with crystallised ginger.

SHEEP SHELTER

Oat Squares

*This tray-bake, made with porridge oats and golden syrup,
is, unusually, flavoured with ginger.*

8 oz. hard margarine	**8 oz. porridge oats**
2 dessertspoons golden syrup	**6 oz. caster sugar**
8 oz. self-raising flour	**Pinch of salt**

2 level teaspoons ground ginger

Set oven to 325°F or Mark 3. Grease a shallow 14 inch x 9 inch baking tin. Gently melt the margarine and syrup in a pan and add to the remaining ingredients in a bowl. Mix well. Put into the tin, spread out evenly and press down firmly with a fork. Bake for 20 to 30 minutes until golden brown. Cut into squares whilst warm and leave in the tin to get cold. Serve either plain or drizzle the top with melted plain chocolate.

Gingerbread Men

A old-time favourite with children of all ages!

4 oz. butter	1 level teaspoon mixed spice
8 oz. self-raising flour	1 tablespoon black treacle
4 oz. soft brown sugar	1 tablespoon syrup
2 teaspoons ground ginger	1 teaspoon orange juice

Set oven to 350°F or Mark 4. Grease and flour baking sheets. Cream together in a bowl, the butter, sugar, treacle, syrup and orange juice. Add the dry ingredients. Knead well with the fingers. Roll out thinly on a lightly floured surface. Make a cardboard gingerbread man (or use a shaped cutter) and use as a template to cut out shapes. Place the 'men' on the baking sheets. Bake for 10 to 15 minutes. Allow to cool for a few minutes before removing from the sheets. Decorate with white and/or coloured glacé icing.

LAZY DAYS

Damson Chutney

This tangy chutney goes well with mature cheese and crusty bread.

3 lb. cleaned damsons   2 pints malt vinegar
1½ lb. Bramley apples, peeled, cored and finely diced
1 lb. onions, peeled and finely chopped
2 teaspoons ground ginger   3 level teaspoons salt
1 oz. pickling spice (tied in muslin bag to handle of pan)
1 lb. soft brown sugar

Put the damsons in a preserving pan with 1 pint of the vinegar and simmer until the fruit is soft enough to remove the stones. When all the stones have been removed and discarded, add the apples, onions, ginger and salt, with the spice bag tied to pan handle for easy removal later. Continue simmering until the mixture is soft then add the rest of the vinegar and the sugar, stirring well until the sugar has dissolved. Continue cooking, until finally when the mixture is thick, remove from the heat. Put into warm, clean jars and seal. Leave to mature for 2 months. Makes about 7 lb. chutney.

Blackberry Cordial

The fruits of the autumnal hedgerows provide this inexpensive and flavoursome drink.

5 lb. blackberries, clean and whole
2 pints cold water   2 oz. citric acid
1½ lb. preserving sugar to every pint of strained juice

Put the blackberries into a large pan and cover with the water and citric acid. Stir frequently, but without breaking or bruising the fruit or the cordial will be dull. Cover and leave to steep overnight. Next day, strain the juice through muslin or a fine sieve into a large saucepan. To each pint of juice add 1½ lbs. preserving sugar. Heat gently, stirring to dissolve the sugar, then bring to the boil and boil for 10 minutes. Leave to cool then strain again into clean bottles with screw tops.

Elderflower Champagne

A refreshing drink to be enjoyed chilled with ice on a hot summer's day.

4 large heads of elderflower (picked on a sunny July day)
1½ lb. granulated sugar
2 pints boiling water
6 pints cold water
Juice and rind of 2 large lemons
2 tablespoons white wine vinegar

Do not wash the elderflowers, but remove any insects and the thick stalks. Put the sugar in a very large bowl and cover with 2 pints of boiling water. Stir until the sugar has dissolved. Then add 6 pints of cold water, the rind and juice of the lemons, the vinegar and the elderflowers. Stir well. Cover, and leave covered for 48 hours, stirring occasionally. Strain through a fine sieve into clean beer bottles with pop-off plastic caps. Leave an inch gap at the top of each bottle and seal. Store in a cool place to mature; the champagne will be ready to drink in 6 weeks.

METRIC CONVERSIONS

The weights, measures and oven temperatures used in the preceding recipes can be easily converted to their metric equivalents. The conversions listed below are only approximate, having been rounded up or down as may be appropriate.

Weights

Avoirdupois	Metric
1 oz.	just under 30 grams
4 oz. (¼ lb.)	app. 115 grams
8 oz. (½ lb.)	app. 230 grams
1 lb.	454 grams

Liquid Measures

Imperial	Metric
1 tablespoon (liquid only)	20 millilitres
1 fl. oz.	app. 30 millilitres
1 gill (¼ pt.)	app. 145 millilitres
½ pt.	app. 285 millilitres
1 pt.	app. 570 millilitres
1 qt.	app. 1.140 litres

Oven Temperatures

	°Fahrenheit	Gas Mark	°Celsius
Slow	300	2	150
	325	3	170
Moderate	350	4	180
	375	5	190
	400	6	200
Hot	425	7	220
	450	8	230
	475	9	240

Flour as specified in these recipes refers to plain flour unless otherwise described.